DEBRIEF THEM

By John Scott

PublishAmerica
Baltimore

© 2009 by John Scott.
All rights reserved. No part of this book may be reproduced, stored in a retrieval system or transmitted in any form or by any means without the prior written permission of the publishers, except by a reviewer who may quote brief passages in a review to be printed in a newspaper, magazine or journal.

First printing

PublishAmerica has allowed this work to remain exactly as the author intended, verbatim, without editorial input.

This publication contains the opinions and ideas of its author. Author intends to offer information of a general nature. Any reliance on the information herein is at the reader's own discretion.

The author and publisher specifically disclaim all responsibility for any liability, loss, or right, personal or otherwise, which is incurred as a consequence, directly or indirectly, of the use and application of any contents of this book. They further make no representations or warranties with respect to the accuracy or completeness of the contents of this work and specifically disclaim all warranties including without limitation any implied warranty of fitness for a particular purpose. Any recommendations are made without any guarantee on the part of the author or the publisher.

ISBN: 978-1-4489-8636-1
PUBLISHED BY PUBLISHAMERICA, LLLP
www.publishamerica.com
Baltimore

Printed in the United States of America

Acknowledgments

A man is not an island all to himself and a good man has several good people behind him, beside him, and with him at all times.

I'd like to first mention my bride, Ramona Scott, who has believed in me even when I couldn't believe in myself. The Lord woke her up one morning and told her to tell me to write a book called "Debrief Them" and as soon as the words escaped her lips I found myself sitting alone at the kitchen table in total silence with pencil and paper while the Holy Spirit started pouring the entire outline for this book into my mind which I transferred onto the paper in front of me in just 15 minutes. By the time Ramona joined me that morning, I had the 92-point outline written and presented it to her. Since she's the more educated one between the two of us and has the ability to organize and type with speed, I gave the written information to her to work her magic on. Through the leading of the Holy Spirit she compiled the 92 points under 5 main headings and organized each point under the proper heading. This became the document I used to complete this book. My sole responsibility was to use the experiences God allowed me to have throughout my life to explain each of the 92 points He had given me through the leading of the Holy Spirit, and then to give all I had written to my bride who was used to complete each point with additional information. Together we have been a team and I thank God He gave me the very one I needed in my life to allow me to be the man both He and she knew I was.

Then I'd like to thank all the people who encouraged me once they found out about the task God had given me to write this book. I thank my counselor, Christian friends and family, my Pastor, Earl Fisher, Jr., sisters and brother-in-law who reside in Flint, Michigan and mainly my big brother Jesus for entrusting this task to me.

Table of Contents

Introduction 9
Book One: Their Thoughts *13*
Don't Set Yourself Up for a Fall 15
Think Rationally 16
Run Your Own Parole 18
Time Stopped, "No!" 19
These Prison Walls 20
Home or Streets 21
But, I'm Back 22
Kick Me Again 23
How People See Me 24
I'm Not Going to Live Long 25
What Should I Think? 26
As a Man Thinks in His Heart 27
I Think I Can Make It from Here 28
The Man! The Man Is You 29
Who Am I? 30
Notes from Book One: Their Thoughts 31
Book Two: Their Actions *33*
Debrief Them: What's This All About? 35
Prison Eyes 36
Picking Up the Pieces 37
Don't Worry, Yours Is Comming 39
Don't Fall 40
Parole Board Dress Rehearsal 41
Follow All the Rules; (Some of Them?) 42
Medication Time 43
Counseling 44
Job Situation 45
You're Not in Prison 46
You Are Out Now 47

Tough Love	48
Church Home	49
I Can't Slow Down	50
Keep Yourself in Check	51
Actions and Attitude Tell	52
Slow Down, Boss	53
Sleep Tight, You're Free	54
You Can't Help Anyone	55
if You're Dead Inside	55
Change Yourself and	56
Everything Around You Will	56
Notes from Book Two: Their Actions	57
Book Three: Suggestions	*59*
Debrief Them: Is This Possible?	61
Don't Strike Her Ever	62
"Game Recognizes Game"	64
Don't Ask Your Mate Anything	66
My Old Buddies	67
Don't Let Your Guard Down	69
She's a Lady, Not a Man	70
Take a Deep Breath	72
Burned Bridges	73
You Earn Respect	74
Cover Up	76
From Boys to Girls	77
Set Mode	78
Dress Normal	79
Con-Out, We Are Not Dumb	80
Let It Go, Turn the Other Cheek	81
Walk Away, He's Afraid of You	82
Notes from Book Three: Suggestions	83
Book Four: Their Feelings	*85*
Debrief Them: Will It Hurt?	87
It Takes One to Know One	88
Sexual Identification	90

True Feelings	92
Off Track; Off My Vision	93
Nothing Makes Sense	94
No Life Expectancy	95
No Room for Hate	96
I'm at My Wits End	97
The Way I See It	98
I Need a Drink	99
Selfish Anger	100
You Are a Changed Man	101
They Haven't Changed; You Have	102
The Woman Looks Good, but I'm Married	103
I Don't Know What's Wrong	104
Now I Have Purpose	105
Notes from Book Four: Their Feelings	106
Book Five: Hope	*107*
Debrief Them: It's What's Needed	109
Love for Self	110
Live for God	111
Everyone Makes Mistakes	112
You're a Jewel	113
I Have a Future	114
Why Can't You Look Me in the Eyes	115
Say You Need Me	117
My Mate Is Still Shy	118
Think About Others	119
Your Children Still Love You	120
You Can Be Anything	121
Those Days Are Over	122
You Are Not Alone	123
God Doesn't Make Trash	125
I'm Only Trying to Help	126
Shake Hands and Come Out Living	127
My Testimony	128
Notes from Book Five: Hope	130

Introduction

There is a debriefing period needed for the ex-offender. They have been through hell and war, and there is a process the mind has to experience in order to prepare the ex-offender to approach life on the other side of the prison bars. A life that will not be what they will expect or fully understand since nothing really stays the same and things do change. The closer it gets to their release date the more their body and mind feels tension because they're not sure what's truly waiting for them. They must be ready for any unpleasant situations from past enemies or prepare themselves for the repercussions they'll face from their significant other, spouse, or children (due to past abuse inflicted on loved ones physically or mentally). If they don't prepare themselves for their release and all they have on their mind is, "freedom," they will not be prepared and can easily be shocked into old habits that will lead them back to prison. They would like to come out taking their rightful place in their homes but soon realize that the family has survived and done all right without them. They would like to get their children to understand that prison isn't "where it's at" and that their children shouldn't do anything that would put them behind bars.

The ex-offender may have depression while at home and may need medication, but he/she isn't aware of it. Without medication they may resort to drinking alcohol or taking drugs. They begin to feel violent because they feel inadequate to their family, spouse, friends, and society in general. They don't have a job and things are not moving as fast as they want or think it should and they don't realize at this point that everything takes time.

The ex-offender needs to be reminded that being free is more than a job or what ever else was lost while being incarcerated. They have to remember that some of their fellow inmates will never get a chance to come home and that they have been given another opportunity to make it out here. And what society needs to know is that when dealing with an ex-offender, 90% of the time only another ex-offender can effectively relate to them and really assist them in their transition as a free person.

What I would like to say to ex-offenders is that they can make it in society as a free man/woman and can stay off drugs and alcohol. They can become anything they have the talent and will-power to become if they have a strong desire to make it happen. I want them to know that they are one of God's blessings to society and they do have a divine purpose. Through joining a Men's/Women's Christian Fellowship group or any type of positive groups in their community, their purpose in life can be discovered and nurtured. Through compassion and love, the void in them can be filled and could bring their life of crime to an end; not just for themselves, but for their family members, too. They need to gain a sense of self-respect and respect for others.

In conclusion, debriefing is an on-going process for as long as it takes each individual to reach their own level of self, assurance, and direction. It's a period where a man or woman can connect with the now, and learn to let go of their past destructive experiences of being locked up, being in a war, or being bound up within their heart and mind for any reason. It's like being in a wheelchair for a certain period of time, and after the physician let you know you're healed enough to not use it anymore, you need to learn to walk all over again without limping, falling, or clumsiness. *Even though the ex-offender may think they are okay, what was instilled in them while being locked up is still there. They have to become aware that the war going on within them is only inside, not outside of them. We need to help them get past the warring going on inside of them and rescue the hidden* emotions that have been pushed down for so long. *They need to be able to see themselves and the world around them as a positive means to gain love, dependence, self-worth, and position. It's all possible.*

II Timothy 2:22 — *Flee the evil desires of youth, and pursue righteousness, faith, love and peace.*

Book One
Their Thoughts

Don't Set Yourself Up for a Fall

Don't put all of your eggs in one basket. What I'm saying is that you can't just depend on others to take care of you or all of your needs, because all these good things must come to an end. Don't depend solely on the system "state programs" to care for you, and only become one of their numbers in their database. This won't help you to learn how to stand on your own two feet.

Always find a job or something to do while living with others. If you can't find a job right off, you can volunteer your services at community agencies (like soup kitchens or missions), or go to a library and read books on anything you want to learn about, as well as get assistance from the librarian to learn how to use a computer. Doing these things show that you are trying to do something different with your life and will make others see you in a different light and cause them to want to help you. While you are volunteering your talents and services, you could end up being noticed by a business owner who may be willing to hire you.

In other words, t*o get something different out of life you have to do something different with your life. You have to prove to yourself and others what you're really capable of achieving. Some of your God-given talents you may not even be aware of until you've made room in your life to experience other things and visit places you normally have not in the past. You won't even realize just how smart you really are until you begin to consume information about things you've only heard of. You can do anything you put your mind and heart to.*

Psalm 32:9 — *Do not be like the horse or mule, which have no understanding*

Think Rationally

Always think with a clear head. You can't think and rationalize things when your mind is influenced by drugs or alcohol. Life can be much better when your sober-minded because you know what you're facing and can make attempts to get through it, not around it only to have to face it again. When you can deal with situations with a clear head and can find ways to get through them, you don't have to worry about the damages you would have caused after you sober up.

Ask questions and find answers. There are no stupid questions, just questions you need understanding on to help you go forward in life. Some of those questions you can answer on your own by first of all being observant of people, places and situations around you, or by using the Internet or a library book.

Use the knowledge that you already have and study about occupations you may want to try out. We all have some special knowledge that have allowed us to gain experience in areas we can share with others. You're grandfather could have plowed fields and taught you how to grow vegetables. Your grandmother could have shown you how to bake cookies from her own recipe. Your teacher could have shown you how to do something particular you can teach others.

After doing something different with your time and efforts and you're still having problems as a sober person, it's all right; you're not by yourself. But you may need to seek professional help if you really have a desire to change your lifestyle. *Everyone has problems; it's how you deal with them that get you through them, not how you dwell on them. Just know that a problem can be solved.*

DEBRIEF THEM

Romans 8:18 — *I consider that our present sufferings are not worth comparing with the glory that will be revealed in us.*

Run Your Own Parole

Be on top of everything. You need to constantly be aware of your surroundings, your own needs, your own issues, and your own appointments so that others don't have to treat you like you need a babysitter. Know that your parole officer is only going to know and be concerned about you the months you are assigned to him/her, but you can do all that's expected of you to get through this parole time. You're smart enough to do this; to get a job, and to stay out of jail or prison. Most of the time you're on parole, the parole officer doesn't have much confidence in you because you're a ex-offender. At times it seems as though they're looking forward to you failing. *You should care enough about yourself to do all it takes to make it. It's your life, not theirs. Don't run, face life head on. Prove to yourself, them, and all of those around you that you have good sense and desire to be the best you possibly can.*

Romans 8:26 — *The spirit helps us in our weakness.*

Time Stopped, "No!"

You think that time stopped while you were incarcerated and you make the mistake of coming out of prison acting like nothing has changed and everyone and everything is the same as when you left. You must realize that time has kept on moving and nearly everything and everyone has changed. Old friends and close relatives have died, and sometimes you haven't been told about it.

Not realizing that things don't stay the same can put a drain on your desire and ability to stay free and could make you feel like you need to go back to old bad habits. You need to face the fact that even the good people you once knew are no longer good, and old places you were once accepted at are no longer there or the atmosphere of those places have changed.

Not even you have stayed the same so you can't expect that anything else has. Your desire should be to make a different lifestyle for yourself so that you don't fall into those same ole places doing the same ole thing and reaping the same ole consequences.

Philippians 3:15 — *All of us who are mature should take such a view of things.*

These Prison Walls

The walls of prison hold you real tight and it seems to squeeze all the life out of you. There was the smell of disinfectant and cigarette butts, the restroom with the doors torn off from fighting or by an angry inmate. The showers are always going to be fixed "next week," with the water running either cold or scolding hot without a warning of which one it will be. Then there's the thing where some inmates take up to 3 showers a day just to get a glimps at the inmates getting off of work and into the showers at the three shifts. If you lay anything down and turn your head, it's gone because if you snooze, you lose and everything in prison is for gain and game.

It takes time to get your thoughts beyond the prison walls, but in time you can and will get past it. This is why you need to take time to focus on anything that will help you get past where you've been. Read, take walks, visit a library, lend a hand at a mission or other assistant agencies; anything that's positive and helps others.

II Timothy 4:7 — *I have fought the good fight, I have finished the race*

Home or Streets

There are times when a person had lost their place in their home before going to prison and they lived on the street (place-to-place, mission, alley, etc.). This will mean that these people will already have a hard time trying to make amends and being accepted back in the door and heart of their family members.

There are some who upon release from prison have already set in their minds and hearts, that they won't be seeing their parole officer and they will most likely end up drinking or going back to the drug of their choice. But this is where it would be beneficial for family or probation officers to encourage and assist the ex-offender to move forward and not backward. They need this type of support from those around them.

The truth is that as we think in our hearts, we will become. *What we look for in life and strive for, we can obtain. The choice is ours, and ours alone.*

James 1:12 — *Blessed is the man who perseveres under trial*

But, I'm Back

With all the sincerity you think you have, you may talk very highly of staying out of trouble because you love and care for your family. The thought is a good thought, but without putting efforts forth to make something different of yourself, it's just a thought that has no foundation.

Yes, it may be very true to think like this, but will thoughts alone stop you from ending up on drugs or back in prison? Did you master your addiction during your time locked up? Loving those you care for is more than just a thought or words. You have to put action behind your thoughts and words to make them true.

Loving your family means that you have the opportunity to finally prove it by doing yourself right and living in a way that benefits you and them.

1 John 2:10 — *Whoever loves his brother lives in the light, and there is nothing in him to make him stumble.*

Kick Me Again

Often times job hunting is hard and you may have to prove yourself by always being up front with the hiring manager, no matter how they will look at you once you have been honest. It's really a let-down when you're not given a chance to prove your work ability and it feels like your being kicked around again and again.

You may especially feel kicked when you haven't been accepted for a job within the first two months of being released, but don't give up. You will have what someone is looking for, and you have to either keep on trying or try something different.

Getting a job is not the only way to make a living. You can go back to school on a college grant, and to find out more information about this all you have to do is go to a local college and talk to a counselor. Or you can start your own business by starting off with small simple things which turn into success in the long run. A couple of examples would be; if you're good at cleaning, clean someone's garage or basement, if you're talent is baking, bake and sell your baked goods in the neighborhood first, then where ever you can. *A good man is knocked down but gets right back up and keeps going.*

Titus 3:14 — *Our people must learn to devote themselves to doing what is good*

How People See Me

People see you by your actions, not what you say. You can say that you can be trusted, but then you'll react out of your hurt and frustrations and do things that cause problems between you and the ones that care about you. You can easily say that you love your family, but your actions prove that you care very little for them.

You just can't come home expecting anything too fast to happen on your behalf. If you try not to expect too much too soon, you won't get too discouraged when things aren't happening at the speed you want them to.

Just slow down, do the best you can because that's all you can do. *Let others see you as someone taking care of business, not someone who's careless, motionless, or selfish.*

Proverbs 14:23 — *All hard work brings a profit*

I'm Not Going to Live Long

There may have been a time in your life when you thought that you wouldn't live long because of the environment you lived in and all the danger around you. You had a few enemies and even thought of yourself as a mighty soldier ready for whatever, when ever, by who ever.

Remember that the way you grew up doesn't have to continue to be who you are. You have choices in life and one of those choices is that you can be what you choose to be with desire and the proper training. Nothing is impossible if you see and believe it that way.

See, you may have lived in the real hood, but get it in your head that you're more than that and remember that God loves you and sees you as more than that.

2 Chronicles 13:12 — *God is with us, He is our leader.*

What Should I Think?

Keep your head up high and your best foot forward. Do what you know to do to get work, food, and other personal needs met. Think positive at all times even when things look unpleasant around you. What you allow yourself to feel inside will give you strength to get through all that's going on outside of you.

By giving everything your best, you'll eventually get the best. By thinking more positively, you gain encouragement to face each day. By taking time to do something different and beneficial for yourself, in time it pays off.

Have faith to believe that *God knows your needs and will supply them according to His riches in glory.*

Isaiah 55:1 — *Come, all you who are thirsty, come to the waters; and you who have no money, come, buy and eat!*

As a Man Thinks in His Heart

You know your limits; try not to go beyond them. Going beyond your limits or biting off more than you can chew can get you in trouble. It can make others see you in a false way and expect something out of you that you won't be able to give them for too long. What's truly in your heart proves who you are.

Only you know if you're cowardly or brave, smart or ignorant, forgetful or have a keen memory? No one knows this better than you and only you can better yourself in the areas where you may be weak. Everyone has some weakness they should be striving to strengthen within themselves. *Trust what you do know and seek after that which you don't know.*

Psalm 71:14 — *But as for me, I will always have hope*

I Think I Can Make It from Here

This is when you begin to think that you don't need God anymore. You know within your heart that you were blessed by God in several ways, but now you're free and can make it on your own. It is so dangerous to think this way since you really don't have control over what life has in store for you. God knows where you've been, where you are right now, and where you're going. Can you really do it alone? *If you're smart, start praying for your needs to be met and believe that it will happen.*

Acts 2:28 — *You have made known to me the paths of life; You will fill me with joy in Your presence.*

The Man! The Man Is You

As an ex-offender, you can defeat your own purpose in life by thinking that you don't measure up to the world's standards. You need to give life your best shot and don't compare yourself to others. You'll be disappointed all the time if you measure yourself by how well others your age are doing, and it can also cause you to get caught up in the wrong things to get fast money and material things.

You know that this will only lead you back behind bars and blaming others for what happens to you. What you become is your choice and has nothing to do with anyone else. *You are your own man.*

Galatians 3:26 — *You are all sons of God through faith in Christ Jesus*

Who Am I?

You are the best thing that God has ever made and He wants you to respect yourself as His greatest creation. God created you for a task that will enhance your life and give you inner and outer happiness above your natural abilities. God is love so He made us to love others and ourselves.

There is no one else exactly like you, and you are special. Be a winner and don't think that just because others seem to move toward their goals quickly, that you're behind. All you can do is just keep moving towards your goal without stopping or being side-tracked.

We all have a gift God gave us that we can continually use to benefit others and ourselves. Once you begin to listen to the voice of God which guides you from within, you will be directed in the right areas of your life. *Just be yourself and always strive to become better.*

II Timothy 2:15 — *Do your best to present yourself to God as one approved, a workman who does not need to be ashamed*

Notes from Book One: Their Thoughts

*Book Two
Their Actions*

Debrief Them: What's This All About?

It is possible to change and become all we can be so that we can make a difference in the world around us. The world around us includes our family, neighbors, friends, and community. It's not so much that we have to prove ourselves to others, but we need to prove to ourselves that we can be the best we can be to better our lives and the lives of all those we hold near and dear to our heart.

In other words, it has got to be for me that I choose a different path in life because this is the only way it would or even could work.

Love starts at home within the heart and then it can be shared with others. We have to first see a need to change, desire to change, then find a way to help make the change. In the end, who we were, who we are, and who we've become affects not only us, but everything and everyone in our lives.

Jude 1:21 — *Keep yourselves in God's love*

Prison Eyes

Even though the ex-offender is out of prison, they may still have one mindset and one way of looking at things. They react to various situations in a way where they won't take the blame or admit their wrong, but will pass on the fault to another person, place, or thing. We all hate to be wrong!

We need to get rid of the scales over our eyes and truly look at ourselves. We see the person we think we are in our own mirror, the one in the looking glass should be you. Only then will you see truth and be real.

We all make mistakes. We make mistakes when we're around others and by ourselves. Some of the mistakes we can laugh at and others we frown about; both are okay because laughing and frowning builds character in a positive way.

Just don't try to be right all of the time, this isn't the way life goes. Many people know this, but don't acknowledge, admit, or act like it's the truth.

Proverbs 14:13 — *Even in laughter the heart may ache, and joy may end in grief.*

Picking Up the Pieces

The ex-offender may really think they will return to society and pick up where they left off. They tell themselves *"I'll just have to move a little faster to get back to where I left off."* Little do they know that the world has changed and people are not the same. Old friends have died and the family and friends homes became parking lots or stores, and all the babies became the grownups now hanging out on the street corners.

Moving fast can be dangerous, so slow down and don't be pushed into moving to fast to get what you don't have. You're free, this should be the first thing on your mind when you wake up until you go back to bed. Living is simple and you can't let the things you can't have right now make you angry and confused. Accept that life is all about taking steps to achieve what you need to survive and strive for your best. If we get hung up on all the things we don't have or can afford right now, we get side tracked.

A job may not be easy to find as soon as you start looking, so you have to learn to live within your means. It should give you a peace of mind that you're free, like a fresh drink of water.

Some other quick advice to ex-offenders who may have a spouse and children to come home to, you don't come home and start asking too many questions about what went on while you were away. Life goes on with you in the picture or without you in the picture and the family didn't cause your absence. If you simply keep your eyes and ears open, it's certain that you'll figure it all out. You've been given another chance to be a part of their lives, don't blow it by allowing your imagination to run wild. Your family may even look at you like you're a stranger, but give it time and it will pass.

Men; don't try to take control over household matters. If you wait it will get handed over to you because you've given it enough time to prove that you're still the man. Home is where you live, it's not the battle zone. When you give everyone around you time to see the changes in you (when you're not trying to hide your true feelings from them) they'll begin to see for themselves who you are. Keep showing and telling them you love them, even when it doesn't seem like they care or are listening. Love conquers all.

1 John 2:24 — *See that what you have heard from the beginning remains in you.*

Don't Worry, Yours Is Comming

The world can't keep a good or changed man down. Everyone should learn from their mistakes, yet, some of us don't. Sometimes it may take a few more downfalls for the ex-offender to realize the truth about life and where they should fit in.

Even I expected too much to happen out here for me as an ex-offender and I thought things would work out like this and go like that, but it didn't. We can't expect too much and we should learn to be satisfied with what ever comes our way.

Accept the simple things like being around loved ones, getting another chance at freedom and another chance to do it better. It doesn't have to be all the 'bling, bling' that you may have been accustomed to. When you set your sights and mind on getting things, you begin to run too fast to get them and you may end up right back in prison. *It's not just about you being free and having a chance to be better, but it's also about those who are in your life.*

1 Peter 3:13 — *Who is going to harm you if you are eager to do good?*

Don't Fall

We need to bring balance in our lives but sometimes we balance the wrong things. We try to straddle the fence in ways like quitting one habit (drinking alcohol) and picking up another habit (smoking weed). But you're telling yourself and friends that you have quit, not admitting to yourself or them that you replaced it with another substance that gets you high.

For me it wasn't weed that kept me in trouble, it was drinking. When it's all said and done, any thing that prevents us from doing what's good and right should be stopped. Alcohol and drugs will bring anyone down sooner or later. *A drug is a drug, and it bites back.*

I Peter 4:7 — *The end of all things is near. Therefore be clear minded and self-controlled so that you can pray.*

Parole Board Dress Rehearsal

There is no dress rehearsal. You're given your appointment to go before the parole board and you go. It's a waste of your time if you don't go in being yourself and being at your best. And even if you do rehearse, once you walk into the stuffy room where the meeting of freedom is going on and the fate of your release date is to be decided; unexpected questions are asked that you wouldn't have even considered. They may ask you if you completed certain programs while being incarcerated, but may not ask another inmate this question.

All you have to remember to do is to know who you are inside and walk in the room with confidence as a reformed man. You've had lots of time to get to know yourself and work on the major issues in your life that landed you in prison. You should have taken advantage of every opportunity to attend all of the programs and classes that could help you reform. This would have been the meaningful thing to do for yourself and to prepare you for your meeting with the parole board.

No matter how hard you try, you can't hide the real you; so you might as well do what it takes to really change your life.

Ephesians 1:18 — *I pray also that the eyes of your heart may be enlightened*

Follow All the Rules; (Some of Them?)

When you are on parole, do what's expected of you. Go to your AA and NA meetings and commit to completing all the other obligations on your parole order. So what if it's a lot of simple things you must do to stay free, it's no different than trying to obtain the level 1 status in prison or getting your opportunity to get paroled. You did what you had to do to get where you wanted to be, it's the same for you out here. *Handle your business!*

Proverbs 14:8 — *The wisdom of the prudent is to give thought to their ways*

Medication Time

Sometimes we are not aware of symptoms of depression (always feeling down), bipolar (continuous mood swings), schizophrenia (multiple personalities), or other mental or personality issues. We think we're okay acting the way we do and depending on liquor and drugs to keep our minds medicated.

God did not create our body and mind to handle alcohol and drugs and our body can't handle the affects of the short and long term damage to the liver, kidney and brain. Yet, we get enslaved to this, sometimes until death.

It's suicide! This isn't the only way to get relief from your pain, illness or troubles. Get help from any one you can or from a medical or counseling facility and/or program.

Seek peace on a daily basis and learn to be okay with yourself. Accept that God made you for His glory so that you may learn to love yourself and others. *Find God in the midst of everything.*

John 6:35 — *Then Jesus declared, "I am the bread of life. He who comes to me will never go hungry*

Counseling

Everyone needs someone to talk to; kings, the president, and other political officials probably have counseling sessions. Don't be ashamed but be smart by making the right decisions in life. "Mums" not the word, share your world with people who are willing to help you understand who you really are. It helps to talk it out so that even you will begin to understand what's really going on within your heart and mind.

When we talk to others we hear ourselves, so get it out on the table. The mess is there no matter how we try to hide it, walk over it, walk around it, or blame it on others. Why not try to look at the mess we've made, sort out why we made it in the first place, why we need to clean it up, and how to go about doing it. *There's help out here, all we have to do is to seek it and we'll find it.*

Isaiah 55:12 — *For ye shall go out with joy, and be led forth with peace*

Job Situation

Being an ex-offender isn't your ticket to getting an entry level job. Try to get your feet in the door of a business, even if it means washing dishes or sweeping the floor. Get your resume ready and list all of your qualifications and past employment experiences. You can sell yourself because there are things that you have done in the past and can do very well.

Have a little faith that some business owner will eventually want to give you the opportunity to prove what you can do, then it's totally up to you to prove how good and reliable you are so that you can move forward in the business once you've been hired.

Even though you've been to prison, not every business owner will hold this against you. Some businesses get tax breaks for hiring ex-offenders.

You just need to be real with them and let them know that you had made some really bad choices in the past that led you to prison, but you've worked hard to change yourself for the better. Let them know that you are accustom to working long hard hours and if you're given the chance to work for them you'll prove to them that you are what they need.

Then let the chips fall where they may because you may get twenty letdowns by being upfront and real, but one day you'll get the "yes" you've been looking for.

Look at it this way; you know what you're capable of being and doing, so it's their loss if they don't want to give you a chance to prove it in their business. *But the lucky business owner that does give you a chance won't be disappointed, especially when you are bound to make him/her proud that he/she hired you.*

Ecclesiastes 11:9 — *Rejoice, O young man, in thy youth*

You're Not in Prison

You are not locked up anymore. Since you are out of prison, why don't you act like it. This means you can come out of the house, visit your friends that don't drink or do drugs, eat what you want, and open the curtains to let the sun shine in the house and in your heart.

You are free indeed, inside and out, mentally and physically; heart, mind, body, and soul. And in Jesus there's freedom to be happy, to love, to be joyful, and to live in peace inside and out. *If you give it a chance, your life can change for the better.*

Isaiah 65: 17 — *For, behold, I create new heavens and a new earth; and the former shall not be remembered, nor come into mind.*

You Are Out Now

The world's rules are different than prison. The world's rules are "do unto others as others do unto you." As an ex-offender your word is a bond and the world doesn't know or understand this about life within the prison walls.

So don't hold those in the world to their word and cause them pain or death because they don't know anything about holding to their word. Just make sure that you are of good stature and look for people with a Christ-like attitude to hang around.

As an ex-offender you have a rooted respect for other ex-offenders that those in the world can never relate to. God understands where we've been and what we need. Don't put any faith in those who don't know or understand.

Do what you need to do to stay free. It's not like you don't know what to do, it's doing it without fear, hesitation and without a doubt that you need to stay free.

Proverbs 14:2 — *He whose walk is upright fears the Lord*

Tough Love

Your family may not say it with words but their actions may be saying "I love you, but there are a few mountains you have to climb first." They need you to prove that it won't be a waste of their time to let you back into their heart and world.

Your bed is hard and you made it that way, so be patient until you find your life. Be of good cheer, the world is watching you and they want to see the real you, not the fake person you thought you had to be. They want to see the person on the inside of you, and whether you think you're showing the real you or not, the real you will always come out.

So why fake it? If you are really trying to better yourself, others will see your intentions and open up a little more every day to allow you to come close to them.

You had to work hard at getting your freedom by being honest and fair. God will bless you gracefully for your willingness to be patient, loving, and kind to yourself first, and then to others. *The reality of it all is that once you continue to be better, others will slowly but surely, little by little, begin to open up to you.*

Joel 1:5, 19 — *Awake, ye drunkards, and weep; O Lord, to thee will I cry*

Church Home

Find love, warmth, and peace within a church where good and kind people attend. There is no perfect church, so go with your heart as to where you feel the most comfortable and accepted.

Once you begin to attend church services your heart will open to let the Word of God shape and mold you into God's perfect instrument. Learn to love the Lord and He will come to you and give you life and peace inside.

Love everyone because with love you can't lose and God will always reward you for doing your part to love even if it seems you're not being loved back. When you spend wasted time hating, you are the loser and can lose your life. Surround yourself with Christ-like people who can be found in the church. *That's why it's important to hook up with a church; who knows, you may find out that you've always belonged to Christ.*

Hosea 14:1 — *O Israel (chosen of God), return unto the Lord thy God*

I Can't Slow Down

Most of the time we let the world give us the run-around. We're always moving and we may be making all the right moves, but we forget about having a balance of things in our lives like sleep, quiet time, and time for self and family. It's okay to handle your business, just remember to slow down to smell the pretty roses you pass on your way to doing your business.

Is your life based on just things and position? Things and position come and go and change constantly; but you have only one life and one time in life to share love with those who are dear to you. *Keep on going, but get your "me time," your family time, and some rest and sleep.*

I Corinthians 10:1,12 — *Moreover, brethren, I wish not that you be ignorant; Wherefore, let him that thinks he's standing, take heed unless he fall.*

Keep Yourself in Check

Always stand outside of yourself and view your real self. Take every opportunity you can to tell yourself how you're worth all the good things out of life. Treat yourself like you're worth it and others will do the same.

Show yourself love today by taking the right steps to get your life together. Concentrate on bettering your life so that even your family member's lives can become better. When you think on yourself and those you love, the love inside of you will free you and cleanse you of the many hurts and pains you've endured and caused.

God loves a contrite (not prideful) and broken heart (admitting your wrong) which shows that we are real with who we are and where we are. *Being real can make and keep you happy.*

Jonah 3:10 — *And God saw their works, that they turned from their evil way*

Actions and Attitude Tell

Acting different won't help you, you have to be different. This means that you have to work out some issues that you have had that caused the pattern that caused you to end up in jail or prison. You know about those issues that caused you to be in bad places; drinking and drugging your mind away and keeping you from knowing wrong from right? The same ole things that keep bringing you back to those same places, feelings, and failures; the same old patterns.

Learn to just take the long way around which means to change your daily routine by filling your day up with a different pattern. Take a walk to the park, run some frustrations off, visit the local library, work at a soup kitchen or volunteer at some community action organization. This is your day so you can do what ever it takes to bring happiness and fulfillment into your life. Set goals by beginning with small ones which will lead to bigger ones in the long run. *You have a purpose in this life, use it.*

Philippians 1:6 — *Being confident of this very thing, that He which hath begun a good work in you will perform it until the day of Jesus Christ*

Slow Down, Boss

Rome was not built in a day and a life can't be built that fast, either. Take things slow enough to think each step out and to make heart-felt decisions. Always check with God about the steps you'd like to take or are already taking and God will open all the right doors for you.

Every door we knock on in life is not always the right door for us. Who knows that better than God? He sees where we've been, where we're going, when we should get there, how to get us there, and how long we are suppose to stay there. So when you try to get something or somewhere and it just doesn't seem to happen, remember that it may not be what will benefit you in the end. *Just don't stop knocking or taking steps towards a better future, have patience to know that in time we'll get there and get what we need.*

Deuteronomy 8:7 — *For the Lord thy God bringeth thee into a good land*

Sleep Tight, You're Free

Relax, slow your mind down, rest, and sleep. Everyone will still be there in the morning. There are no guards, no wake up calls for breakfast, or work detail. You've made it home and now have the opportunity to make something of yourself. Make your plans on what you need to do to get where you need to be mentally, physically, and financially. *This is your time in your life to make yourself proud.*

Hebrews 4:3 — *For we which have believed, do enter into rest*

You Can't Help Anyone if You're Dead Inside

Stay in good cheer, stir it up within so that others see you and can see the shining light you are becoming. They will begin to see God in you through all you do and say. If you are living then life is not lost. Every new day represents a new opportunity to better your life. God does have a purpose with you in mind and no matter what happens on a day-to-day basis in this life, God is in control and won't let you fail at all of your intentions. No matter how hard it may seem, bite your lip and take the ride on through life. Pray at all times and get some of God's Word in you. *This will help to change the foundation of your life from worthless to worth more than can be imagined or dreamed.*

II Peter 1:2 — *Grace and peace be multiplied unto you through the knowledge of God, and of Jesus our Lord.*

Change Yourself and Everything Around You Will

When a person changes their pattern of life and make changes for the better, the right and good things will begin to happen. Change the old pattern of going to the bar, dealing with old worldly friends, and being selfish and selfless. Instead, go to church, get new godly friends, put others before yourself, and think more highly of yourself than you use to.

The Lord does His best work through Christ-like people, those who know and understand that they don't have to endure (put up with) long suffering for too long, because joy comes in the morning for them that believe it will. You can keep your joy no matter what the evil in the world tries to prove. *When you have joy inside, evil can't take it away.*

Philemon 1:20 — *Yea, brother, let me have joy of thee in the Lord*

Notes from Book Two: Their Actions

*Book Three
Suggestions*

Debrief Them: Is This Possible?

It is possible to change and become all we can be so that we will make a difference in our lives, the lives of our family members, and become upright citizens in our communities.

It's time to know and accept that we didn't become criminals over night and we won't become the best we can truly be over night. It takes dedication, determination, willingness, and good intentions on our part to do all we can do to be all we can be. We've tried the other way; getting things fast and dirty and paying for it with our lives.

Let's try God's way and be the great creations He designed us to be. It's not impossible and we're worth the best out of life that we can achieve.

Hebrews 6:12 — *That ye be not slothful (slow moving), but followers of them who through faith and patience inherit the promises.*

Don't Strike Her Ever

Men can sometimes look at the woman as the weaker sex and some men take this to the extreme and perform acts of violence and rape on women. Men need to look at the overall picture and say "God made woman a helpmate to the man, Adam, to care for the garden and be his companion." By hurting her, we're hurting ourselves since she's apart of us. Flesh of man's flesh and bone of his bones.

But, out of wedlock comes Satan who brings strife into a relationship and all types of calamity (problems) on couples. Satan attacks in the weak areas of relationships and uses a couple's weaknesses to break down and tear a part family and home.

And where troubles really build is when the couple is living in thoughtless sin where one or both are deceiving, cheating, hefty gambling, or over-use of drugs and alcohol. When involved in this type of destructive behavior, things may go right for a season but in the end it's always the same; fighting, breakups, financial problems, and death.

Marriage is more than two people speaking words at a ceremony, marriage is a covenant vow! If a couple looks at their union as a covenant, it's hard for the enemy to penetrate it because the marriage is ordained by God and has Christ-like love (unconditional love).

You don't strike someone you love and you don't take their dignity, sense of self-worth, or pride and joy away from them. A covenant is a agreement by the man and woman that they will honor and love each other until death do them apart. They put each other first, which means that neither of them will lack any good thing because they're caring for each other.

Don't hit her; hug and encourage her, instead. You wouldn't break your own ribs on your physical body, so why would you damage the flesh and bone that God took from your body? "God put Adam to sleep and removed one of his ribs and formed woman."

Hebrews 13:1,4 — *Let brotherly love continue; Marriage is honorable in all*

"Game Recognizes Game"

As an ex-offender you may think that just because you've been incarcerated, you can still get over on the system and any person who crosses your path. What you need to realize is that you are the one who has been away and while you were away things changed on the outside. The people and systems you use to scam, got wiser and better, so look out!

Time didn't freeze while you were locked up, and just because you could scam your way to get a few soaps and soups in prison doesn't mean you can scam your way through life on the outside. You've been out of touch with the real world and all of the changes that have taken place, so even if you think you're a hustler, you're only a jail-time hustler.

You need to change and try the truth from now on. It's not easy to change your way of thinking, but once you see that your old scamming ways don't get you anywhere, maybe you'll try the truth to see if that might work.

Do you actually think you're not being watched by everyone everywhere you go? When everyone's eyes are on you and focused on your actions and attitude and wondering about your intentions, you become as a glass object shining on the outside but dirty on the inside. Don't you know that when you try to hide behind lies and deception, you're going to slip up sooner or later and reveal your true intentions and motives.

In other words, if you're still smoking cocain, almost every cocain addict can tell that you're smoking no matter what you may say, dress like, or do to play it off.

DEBRIEF THEM

The finger is pointed; family and friends are not fooled by our intent to con and manipulate them out of anything. So you might as well come with the real. Sooner or later the real you surfaces no matter how hard you try to keep it hidden.

I Samuel 26:23 — *The Lord render to every man his righteousness and his faithfulness*

Don't Ask Your Mate Anything

Let's say that someone was incarcerated for 5 years, came home to spouser and children, and the first thing they did was play detective and start asking too many questions about what went on while they were gone?

First of all, why does someone want to come home and dig up old information? Are they hoping to hear some bad news so that they can use it as the perfect excuse to go out, get high, or hurt someone?

Second of all, you can't begin to tell your family what your life was behind bars, why would you expect to fully know what their lives were truly like while you were locked up?

Third point would be that even if your family could tell you word-for-word and action-for-action of everything said and done every hour you were gone, what could you do with that information since you can't change what was said and done? You can't even use the information to make a difference in the outcome of what everyone said or did while you were away.

The truth can hurt so just be cool and roll with the punches because asking questions will only hurt. Let your mate tell you what they want you to know. Lighten up on needing to know everything. Anyway, if you just pay attention to what's going on in your family right now, you'll figure out the missing pieces of each family member's life that is necessary for you to know and react to.

Life didn't stop just because you weren't around. *All you really need to know is how to get your life on the right track so that you can stay free inside and outside (mentally, emotionally, spiritually, and physically).*

I Corinthians 3:19 — *For the wisdom of this world is foolishness with God.*

My Old Buddies

Do not, (I stress this point), start hanging out with all your old pals who are still doing the same ole thing the same ole way and are still stuck in that meaningless way of life. It's not that you're trying to be stuck-up or make them feel like you're better than they are; it's just that you need to do what it takes to make your life better and in the process, maybe they'll pick up on some of your new habits and follow your lead.

When you begin to think right and do the right things, you're setting an example for others to follow. At first your pals may think that you're just trying to be too good for them, but once they see the right things begin to happen for you, they'll see you a little differently. Instead of allowing them to influence you in the wrong way, you can influence them in the right way.

One of the main reasons you need to be cautious is because once you get around old pals and familiar grounds, you may get relaxed and listen to them as they say things like "You're a man, have a drink, after all, you use to be a drug addict, not a alcoholic," and get side tracked or pulled from your efforts of making your life better. If they can turn your focus on old habits and you begin to think thoughts like "one won't hurt me"; as they watch you drink they'll bring out the drugs so that you'll be just like them.

You've got to do what it takes to keep yourself free, healthy, and out of trouble.1 You've got to be an example of a better way, a better lifestyle, and a more successful future. Even if you have to change friends for a while until they accept you for bettering yourself, there are other people you can hang out with.

Try getting some Christian or college pals, anyone who will be a good positive influence in your life and the lives of your loved ones. Anyone who can encourage you and be willing to give you a hand in making your life better.

Ephesians 1:17 — *That the God of our Lord Jesus Christ, The Father of glory, may give unto you the spirit of wisdom*

Don't Let Your Guard Down

Always leave yourself something to do so that you don't fall into thinking and day-dreaming about things that will cause you stress or worry, like what you don't have. Where you're suppose to be you'll be and what you're suppose have is coming.

Just take your time and stay on your plan of action that will lead you towards a better future. All that you need will come sooner or later, but if you don't always have something to do you'll fall right back into your old self again. If you allow that, everything you've strived to do becomes nothing and meaningless. Then the guilt will begin to eat you alive and catapult (throw) you right back into the streets where you may stay until you do something that causes you get locked up again.

That's why you have to keep yourself busy doing something, whether it's spending the day putting in applications, sitting at the library reading, or attending church services (bible studies, prayer, fellowship). Taking walks or exercising are things you can also do. *I'm sure you can think of something positive to keep yourself active and out of trouble.*

I Peter 5:6 — *Humble yourselves, therefore, under the mighty hand of God.*

She's a Lady, Not a Man

As a male ex-offender, being in a all-men's institution for any amount of time (1 to 20 years), we realized that even though we're men, we still have certain needs for companionship, attention, and a need to be held. Many of us were not fortunate enough to get this from our home life and we even searched for it in certain women, only to find out that a woman couldn't fulfill or understand we had a need to be held compassionately as a mother holds her baby, making a soul connection instead of just a regular relationship that the world has to offer.

At times men may begin to think that another man knows what they need in a relationship, and being in the prison system, the same-sex relationships look happy and normal for this setting. But, it's all just a selfish need going over board. You're not being judged in this comment because just as my words in this book try to point you in a more constructive and meaningful way of life, these words in this section are intended to do the same. No one can tell others how to live, but it's okay to advise and direct others who may desire or be seeking to do things differently.

What may not be realized at the time the need arises to just be touched, held, and adored by someone is that it's really just a case of loneliness that can be dealt with in so many other ways than homosexuality. We all get lonely behind bars, but there's other ways to relinquish (release) this infidelity with another man.

Keep your mind and hands busy doing something to better yourself (reading, writing, attending services, exercising, attending classes the prison may offer, or find work). Read James 1:7 and count it all joy when going through the loneliness of prison; and make real friends, not sex partners. Once you're touched in the wrong way, the door is open for Satan to come in to steal, kill, and destroy.

Be of good cheer and learn to love and be loved in the right way, God's way.

Galatians 6:7 — *Be not deceived; God is not mocked; for whatsoever a man sows (does), that shall he also reap (get)*

Take a Deep Breath

Life is full of surprises, and most of the time these surprises can catch you off guard with all types of ways we don't want to deal with right now or ever. But procrastination (not doing something right now) is not a good ally (friend) to be dealt with so you need to take care of your business before it takes care of you.

Smile and try to stay happy at all costs so that you don't give a foothold to the devil and get side-tracked into stepping into trouble. All you'll be showing the devil by doing what's necessary to stay heppy, is that you're up when you're suppose to be down and you're smiling when you're suppose to be sad.

Take a deep breath and follow your heart, and God will carry you the rest of the way through each day. You're out of prison, you are free, and you're alive. There are those who didn't make it out or didn't wake up this morning. *Be blessed and dare to dream, think, love, and be happy.*

Romans 12:18 — *If it be possible, as much as lies in you, live peacefully with all men.*

Burned Bridges

What is a burned bridge? It's a worn out welcome through hurts and pains that we may have caused someone and we may or may not realize it. We may not understand that we're played out with friends and family because they don't want to be hurt and disappointed by us anymore, and if we do understand, we're just not caring that we're wearing out our welcome.

A burned bridge may not be crossable anymore and the people we hurt may be totally finished with us, our behaviors, and our patterns of destruction. And even if we're changing or changed on the inside, we may not get the chance to prove it because the scars we caused were too deep.

The only thing you can do is to keep moving in the right direction and stay focused on your plan of action to a better future. Bridges can be repaired in time once it's taken some time for it to be proven that you can be trusted again.

Give others you've hurt a chance to see you from a different light and they may let you back into their hearts and lives. *Time can heal wounds.*

I Peter 3:8 — *Finally, be of one mind, having compassion for each other*

You Earn Respect

The world doesn't owe us anything because we were locked up in mind, body, and soul. We owe it to ourselves to walk uprightly as a changed person with some direction. We are known by the fruit we bare; meaning that people know us by our actions. Actions don't just happen, there's a thought first, and then we react to that thought. Most people know that what you do and say comes from your heart, so if you're acting ugly, you're a messed up person on the inside; and if you're acting like you have some sense, you're getting it straight on the inside.

Your fruit also comes from the seeds you plant; meaning that if all you've shown others is that you don't have it together and is constantly hurting yourself and those around you, this is all they'll believe about you. Good fruit is your good, positive, and loving behavior you show by doing yourself and others right. If you don't want people looking at you half-heartedly as an ex-offender, (which is smart on their behalf if you haven't changed), you have to change and give them something different to believe about you.

We can't expect to come out of prison and immediately get the respect we may think we deserve after abandoning spouse, children, job and friends. Sometimes if you've had a chance to work on your relationships with spouse and children while you've been locked up, this may not be a problem upon your release. But often times this doesn't happen. So, as the family may see it, we gave them up for our moment of sin with the consequence of incarceration. What we need to realize is that we need to concentrate on showing respect to our own self and others will have to respect us, too. *That's why we have to make a difference in our own life, which is how we show that we respect ourselves.*

I John 3:7 — *Little children, let no man deceive you; he that does righteousness is righteous*

Cover Up

It's really not a good thing when we spend more time trying to hide our negativity than actually doing the negative deed. We lie to our parole officer about our "no-shows," to family about drinking and drugs, to our boss, and to friends. Why even start lying, knowing that the end results will be broken homes, destruction, and defeat?

Yes, you're going to think about drinking and drugs; why not, you're still in recovery. If you're not doing what it takes to get over it you'll be influenced daily to see if you still have an appetite for it. That's to be expected, but you can overcome daily temptation by doing what it takes to change on the inside. You have to be real with yourself and with counselors when you're struggling in these areas of your life. There is help, and people are willing to be there for you if you want them to. *Help can't be forced on you, you have to want it. So, want to change and get the help you need.*

Hebrews 3:13 — *But exhort one another daily, while it is called today*

From Boys to Girls

When an inmate has a same-sex relationship while in prison, there's a transition that takes place once they are released from prison. They may lose their normal thought pattern of their true sexual identity and find it hard to connect back to their different-sex mate on the outside. They may believe in themselves that they may never measure up to being a full-fledge man or woman again behind closed doors.

Knowing that they have selfishly indulged in a relationship while in prison, they may feel the guilt and shame of this and may not be able to share this with their mate in all truthfulness. They may trick themselves into believing that the inmate they fooled around with was really the opposite sex, but knowing deep down inside this wasn't true. This mind game is played while behind prison walls and when the transition is made to leave prison for home, the desire to be with the same sex may not surface again while on the outside.

The problem is that the thoughts of what was done with a mate while you were incarcerated is going to be there like a bad dream, and this can cause a relationship with a spouse or significant other to fall short of it's full potential once you're back home; all because of the sexual acts that were committed while being locked up just to satisfy selfish needs.

There is forgiveness and freedom found in God who can clean your heart and mind and make you whole and happy.

I John 3:1 — *Behold what manner of love the Father has bestowed on us, that we should be called the sons of God*

Set Mode

Often we say, "Well that's just me and I'm set in my own ways." No, you're set in a selfish way that is hurting you and others. You have to learn how to bend a little bit towards someone else's way of doing and thinking about things. It may hurt a little at first, but it'll feel better if you let it.

When you do the same thing the same way day in and day out, that only becomes a job; and why work all day? Change up, have some fun and don't follow the same pattern you have always followed. Slow down and don't be obsessive over anything because obsession can lead to a bad disposition (outlook on life). Set a mode of good standards. Live and let live. *A set mode takes up 24 hours a day; take 12 of those hours to have some fun and change your pattern.*

Jude 1:21 — *Keep yourselves in the love of God, looking for the mercy of our Lord Jesus Christ unto eternal life.*

Dress Normal

Be who you are and know that it does matter how you wear your clothes; pants past your butt don't give a good representation of your motives to better yourself. The way you dress not only reveals what you feel about yourself, but it shows how much respect you have for yourself and those around you. It also shows what your attitude is towards life and towards others.

It's simple; the way you feel is definitely the way you dress and act. Your mouth will say, "I want something more out of my life," but your actions and the way you dress says the complete opposite. If you want the employer to hire you, you don't dress like you're stepping out to the dance club to pick up somebody; you dress like you want the employer to think of you as someone who means business and wants to make something of yourself.

Another reason to dress better is to set a good example for those around you so that they can follow your lead. *By bettering your life, you better the lives of those around you.*

I Timothy 4:12 — *Don't let anyone look down on you because you are young, but set an example*

Con-Out, We Are Not Dumb

When coming out of prison you might think friends and family may be like they use to. It's highly unlikely that trust and honor will still be there, these are things that you would have to earn back from them because you not only hurt yourself by going to prison, but you hurt them, too. It's the ripple effect of your actions where you hurt yourself by being locked up and you hurt the ones who love you by what you did.

Your family dealt with embarrassment within their community and they even had to deal with what others thought like when they looked at your family, knowing they were wondering what's in your bloodline (family line) that would produce someone like you? These are the feelings you've come home to, and as long as you prove yourself to be much more than they remembered you as, the hurt feelings, distrust, and un-forgiveness will break in most of your family and friend's hearts. *But for those who won't allow themselves to see the changed you, you just have to keep focusing on what you need to be doing to get where you need to be.*

1 Peter 5:10 — *But the God of all grace, who has called us unto His eternal glory by Christ Jesus, after we have suffered a while, make you perfect, established, strengthened, and settle you.*

Let It Go, Turn the Other Cheek

My friend, no matter how smart you think you are, don't argue at every pointed finger at you. The more you can endure of the world and all its persecution, God will give you more of Himself to help you get through the circumstances at hand. You will become mighty in mind, body, and soul without reproach (pointed fingers). "Turn the other cheek," does not mean that you should let someone beat you down or hurt you physically; *it means that you should find other ways of solving your differences by using love and respect, and positive means possible.*

I John 3:18 — *My little children, let us not love in word or in tongue; but in our deeds and in truth*

Walk Away, He's Afraid of You

At times friends, loved ones, and other people we've harmed while in our wrong state of mind, are unsure and afraid of us, especially since we're ex-prisoners back in their society. Keep in mind that they are not aware that the prison system has changed drastically since the early 1950's and 1960's when the only thing prisoners had as amusement was someone hanging themselves, being apart of or watching a fight, or a inmate getting raped in the showers.

Now that we're in the latter days, things changed for the better and prisoners have a choice on whether to engage in negative acts or to excel in some or all of the programs that are available within the prison system. By deciding to do the right things, it builds a sense of self-worth and raises your self esteem which was probably missing when you were first incarcerated.

Idol hands is the devils workshop and prisoners want to go home these days, so rape and fighting aren't on their agenda. Most of those who held down jobs and participated in school projects think with a clear head and apply everything they've learned to give them a more positive lifestyle on the outside of the prison walls. And in the heart of those bettering themselves while being locked up, they don't plan on returning to prison again. That's why you just have to walk away from those who have their false perception of what they heard or perceive a prison life is all about. They act the way they do towards you because they are afraid of you and they don't understand anything about you or your desire to move forward in life. *Just give society time to see a changed person, and they will learn to love and respect you again, in time.*

Philippians 2:4 — *Look not every man on his own things, but every man also on the things of others.*

Notes from Book Three: Suggestions

Book Four
Their Feelings

Debrief Them: Will It Hurt?

Change is not easy, but it's a constant part of everyone's life. Some changes just automatically take place, whether we're prepared for them or not. Other changes happen because we take the right or wrong steps to make them happen, which results in either good or bad changes on our part.

A good change would result from doing some positive things to keep you motivated and stimulated to learn. Like going to a library and beginning to read books on all types of subjects. The change that would take place is that you grow in knowledge and begin to know and understand many things.

Another way change happens is when you allow yourself to see truth instead of believing in the lies that have kept you in trouble, angry, unforgiving, or unhappy for years. The more positive influence in your life, the more the truth is revealed and the more sense is gained over what you thought you knew.

Change isn't always easy but it is necessary when you want your life to be more than it has been. To get something different out of life we all have to do something different. You can't get something different to happen in your life by continuing to do the same things the same way. Nothing changes if you continue to see the same people who are up to no-good, act the way that has kept you going nowhere in life, or leaning on others to be responsible over you.

Who knows, once you allow yourself to make something more out of your life, you may just like it.

Philippians 1:6 — *Being confident of this very thing, that He who began a good work in you will perform it until the day of Jesus Christ*

It Takes One to Know One

    Some physicians think their attempt to reach the ex-offender with a alcohol abuse problem will work, but this is not always true. First of all, a alcoholic has to have their own reason to quit. It can't be for the children, wife, mother, or any other person's sake in his life.

    Alcoholism is stronger than the love you have for your loved ones, and if you haven't had your own personal reasons for quitting, you'll end up back on the merry-go-round going through the same emotional trauma alcohol and/or drugs takes you through. You drink, act a fool, spend all your money, have to face the drama at home because of it, feel like a failure again, promise to quit again, and be at it again in the next few days. Around and around you go on that merry-go-round that takes you nowhere.

    Life should be more like a roller coaster. We have our down times, but we know that you'll be going up again. This is okay because how would we know when we're up if we've never experienced being down? Or how would we be able to relate to others when they're down if we've never been there?

    The only hope for you is to bring out the square person within you that lies dormant most of the time because you have your reputation to portray. Bring forth the spirit that only God can activate within a person, and then you may find a reason to stay sober.

    Some things worthwhile that will keep your mind off of your habits is: helping others find their better way in life, leading others to Christ, visiting prisoners to bring them hope of a better future, or talking to others about the effects of alcohol and drugs. By talking about it in a positive setting, the ex-offender may build more confidence within himself at every opportunity taken to talk and help others.

Your experiences are seeds you can plant into others to watch truth and life spring forth.

Philippians 4:5 — *Let your moderation (self control) be known unto all men.*

Sexual Identification

Young people come to prison basically understanding their sexual identity, but somewhere they lose themselves and become something they aren't. They change their sexual identity for some badly-needed attention, and if they feel no one is really caring if they even exist, life becomes a game and a movie scene where they have the only part to play and can invite the ones they choose to play this game and part with them.

Because they need attention, fellow prisoners will tell them how pretty they are so that they can eventually act that part. And because they're finally getting some much-needed attention and because they desire companionship, this will eventually lead into sexual relationships. These sexual relationships will begin to confuse their mind and cause them to forsake their true sexual identity only to eventually get passed around like a bar of soap.

That person is finally getting the attention they sought out, because other prisoners will want to take showers with them. This may just last until they connect with someone they can trust enough to lead them down the right path; someone who may be able to break through all the confusion and give them some spiritual enlightenment.

God made us all self-sufficient; needing only self to find true love, joy, happiness, and life from within, not from the outside until we realize that it was within us all the time. We can be attentive to our own needs and learn how to care for ourselves, not depending on others to give us a reason to have good hygiene, eat right, and just simply enjoy being alive. We can even keep ourselves amused without anyone being around us by playing a card game, learning to play an instrument, write stories or poems, or read books.

Anyone can leave homosexual acts and be forgiven by God once they've left that lifestyle. But they will also need to forgive themselves and begin to pray and witness to others who are still indulging in such acts.

James 2:12 — *Speak and act as those who are going to be judged by the law that gives freedom*

True Feelings

The ex-offender may not know they are suffering from neglect, like a trustee who the guards are not treating like other inmates, making him complete obscene task as a porter or kitchen assistant; taking away some of their dignity without them even being able to express their dislike of the treatment. There may still be some animosity (anger) there because of this mistreatment and they don't know how to express it.

This anger is misplaced and released on or at someone weaker than themselves and is even expressed beyond the prison walls. And when this happens, there can be trouble.

And there are those ex-offenders who had great friendships or a homosexual relationship while locked up and they miss this so much that they commit some silly crime just to get back there. They may need medical help but not realize that they need it. They could be suffering from severe depression, bi-polar tendencies, mental illness or something else; and unless they're screened and diagnosed as soon as possible, they suffer and cause suffering. Some may even adjust to prison life and to them it seems the perfect life even with their underlying problems. With 1-on-1 counseling there can be help, as long as the ex-offender feels they can trust someone and connect with them. Even a group session is good when there are people with similar experiences and problems discussing them. *In other words, there's hope and help if you seek for it.*

Matthew 7:7 — *Ask and it shall be given to you; seek, and ye shall find; knock and it shall be opened unto you*

Off Track; Off My Vision

Stay on track at all times by doing what's best for you and for your own happiness. There are many distractions waiting for you and at times it seems that nothing goes the way you expect it to. Have a vision of who and what you want to be in your heart and mind, and even if you get off course from your vision and out of the will of God, God's blessings are upon your vision and the sun will eventually shine through to direct you to accomplish your vision.

Life unravels into a clear and wonderful life, especially when your attending your AA meetings, group sessions, 1-on-1's, and church meetings. We all need help at times and God will put good people in your life to lend you a helping hand. Even the angels of God assist you in your life endeavors (plans). I believe that heaven rejoices when you obtain gladness within yourself. As long as you're being honest and truthful, and fight for what's right, God will make sure you achieve the things you want to achieve. *What you believe in your heart and speak out about yourself will come true. Keep the vision.*

III John 1:11 — *Beloved, don't follow that which is evil, but that which is good, He that does good is of God*

Nothing Makes Sense

Things only start making sense when we let go and let God do the driving down each road of our lives. God knows the beginning and ending of our life's story. He looks upon the heart and blesses us according to the deeds of our heart. It's from the heart that we do good deeds or bad deeds. It's the heart that dictates what we say and do which means it influences our mind and actions. So we should do all things with a good heart motive and with all confidence that if we do, all will fall in place in our lives.

Some days it seems nothing makes much sense, usually because we're trying to do our own thing and it doesn't turn out right. Could it be that it's not right because we really don't know what's ahead like God does? And what looks right to do at the moment would cause big problems and unnecessary pain and stress in the future. God has all the answers and can direct us to and through the right doors in our lives. We're responsible for taking care of ourselves, learning more, eating right, exercising to stay healthy, looking for work, volunteering our talents to help others, *and depending on God to put us where we need to be and giving us what we need when we get there.*

Revelation 21:4 — *And God shall wipe away all tears from their eyes*

No Life Expectancy

Some ex-prisoners lived in a community that was like living daily in a battle zone, and they didn't think they would live long enough to worry about what life would be like at a certain age. When there are thoughts like that, they don't think they have a need to learn, to change, or to try not to be the doggie dog they're known to be. They have to maintain their hate mode so that they don't have to have the feelings that won't allow them to continue to thug and do wrong with no regrets.

They think that nothing really matters and if they end up in prison or dead, it won't mean anything because others will go down with them. This type of thought pattern is hard to deal with and until they can actually see a reason to think differently, they can't and they won't. There needs to be a strong role model for them to observe before they'll consider a different way of seeing and living life. This is where a good mentor would come into play; someone who's come out of the same lifestyle and has obtained a different status in life; someone who can totally relate to them on their level of knowledge and understanding. *When we finally do realize what life can really be, we need to share with those still seeking.*

Philemon 1:7 — *Your love has given me joy and encouragement, because you, brother, have refreshed the hearts of the saints.*

No Room for Hate

Hate will eat you inside out and make you go to an early grave. You may not think too highly of yourself and others at times, but you can rise above hate when you realize that the ones you hate are living their lives while you're choking the life out of yourself with hatred towards them.

The best way to get even with someone who has hurt you is to show them that you've moved on in life and you are trying to make something of yourself, regardless of how hard they may have tried to stop you. It doesn't work well for any of us when we believe that we're suppose to do unto others as they do unto us. Somewhere hate has to come to an end so that it doesn't transfer into our children.

Holding on to hate is like renting an apartment and living on the street in the winter months. Just go on into your apartment and get the warmth waiting for you. In other words, get the warmth that love gives so that you can live a longer, happier life. *God didn't create us to hate, this came from the pits of hell where hate wants to send you.*

I John 5:3 — *This is love for God: to obey His commands*

I'm at My Wits End

It feels like everything goes wrong at the same time. You come home from prison to find that your mate is standoffish, the job situation was going nowhere, and it's all on your shoulders to get all you need to get on your feet. You have to build up your wardrobe, try to keep yourself mentally stable to get through the day, try to get others to see you as more than an ex-prisoner, and at times you even have to come home and become the mediator between family disputes (disagreements).

Don't allow yourself to feel worthless, just focus on what you need to do each day to accomplish some of your goals. Even if you have to wear the same pair of pants 2 days in a row before you get something else to wear, be happy that you're in the position to get out there and get what you need. Keep in mind that this isn't an instant life and we don't get everything right now, but with patience and persistence (never giving up), we can get what we need and end up where we need to be. *The world isn't running out of money, and more importantly, we need to nurture (hold on to) the good relationships we have with friends and family which give us strength to conquer everything else.*

Revelation 21:7 — *He that overcometh shall inherit all things*

The Way I See It

You only have one life, so live it to the fullest and to the best of your ability. Not according to the way someone else expects you to live it. When you've come from having nothing, you're more grateful with everything you work to get. You have to know that your blessings will come to you because a good man can't be kept down. Especially when you handle disappointment with a good attitude, the devil doesn't know where else to hit you when you just keep on smiling and moving forward.

You deal with life's ups and downs lightly and equally, and you realize that everyone has ups and downs. Anyway, your trials only turn into experiences in the long run. That's the way I see it.

I John 4:4 — *Ye are of God, little children, and have overcome them; because greater is He that is in you, than he that is in the world.*

I Need a Drink

If at all possible you should find another way to stir up joy inside of yourself. Drinking is only a way to feel happy for a short time before you do or say something stupid to ruin the moment of happiness. You also have to worry about doing something wrong under the influence of alcohol that would cause your life to be taken or put you back behind bars.

Why take that chance? You're smarter than that, you're not a total fool. Accept it; you can't drink anymore without causing more problems on top of the ones already created because of your drinking problem. You may even tell yourself that you need a drink to come down to earth and relax, or you need a drink to take the load off. Drinking causes you to take a vacation from real life, but it also causes your life to begin to fall apart into pieces (affecting your emotions and mind).

At times it can cause you to be unaware of your surroundings, your friends to pull back from you, losing your job, and lose your mate. You'll feed yourself messages like, "it's okay because I'll get another job and I'll get my loved ones back." This is a dream, and without true happiness there's no chance of joy. *Being sober may not be an easy choice to make, but when you can face life with a sober mind, at least you can justify (make sense of) your choices and behaviors.*

II Peter 2:9 — *The Lord knows how to deliver the godly out of temptations*

Selfish Anger

When we're holding anger against someone, it may be a way of saying, "I don't want to be bothered at this time." The anger that's being felt is selfish and there's no room for outsiders. The anger is only removed by careful love and attention slowly given to you by others; not overdone love (smothering), but leaving room for the anger to die down like a forest fire being put out.

Sometimes the anger is an attempt to keep others at a distance so that there's no room to be hurt or disappointed. *An angry person is really a compassionate person inside; one who can cry at a movie scene or be moved by watching children play. They're someone who really cares deeply about many things but will only show this side to someone who moves their heart.*

James 4:10 — *Humble yourselves in the sight of the Lord, and he will lift you up*

You Are a Changed Man

Some ex-offenders may think that they really haven't changed much while they've been in prison, but they don't realize that they really have. Change is a natural part of life and God created us to bring about change in the world. While in prison you learned the respect-system where you learned to listen without any argument and realized that it's better to earn respect than to fight for it. You found that there was another way, and without knowing it you even carried this attitude outside of the prison walls.

It's important that others see that change in you to make them realize that the prison system can produce changed attitudes that prevent so us from returning to prison. *We ex-offenders must keep on changing and improving our horizon (future) and continue to use our minds to stay on track of our vision.*

Colossians 3:23 — *And what you do, do it with your whole heart, as unto the Lord, and not unto men*

They Haven't Changed; You Have

When we are released from prison and arrive home, things are somewhat different. The children are shy, your mate shows little compassion towards you, and your family has changed their lifestyles. We begin to feel tension because no one seems to want to get too close to us because of the person they remember us to be. They haven't changed in their way of thinking about us, but we have to know within ourselves that we have changed.

With the help of God, and in time, they will begin to see the changes in us, especially when we allow Jesus Christ to change us from the inside out (known as a born-again Believer). When this happens, our outward appearance begins to match our inward change and even our eyes begin to sparkle and show unspeakable joy. *You have changed, and without words your actions will show it. All will be fine and your new life will begin to look and smell like sweet roses.*

Colossians 2:13 — *And you, being dead in your sins and the uncircumcision (uncleanness) of your flesh, has he quickened together with Him, having forgiven you of all your trespasses (wrong doings)*

The Woman Looks Good, but I'm Married

Always make your spouse your royal mate and your dream-come-true. Especially if they've been there for you through all the crap they had to experience and endure from you. When no one else (including yourself) respected you, they did and even took care of you when you had no one else that would.

They've been there when you needed them the most. Every other person who looks good to you may not have your best interest at heart and only want you to fill a selfish need they may have, making you look like a fool in the end. It's the one that has proven their love and dependability (can count on them) that you need to keep steady in your life.

If they haven't gone anywhere yet, do all it takes to give back to them the same respect and love. You may even want to try to adore them more than they have adored you.

Ephesians 5:33 — *However, each one of you also must love his wife as he loves himself*

I Don't Know What's Wrong

Sometimes we can't see all the way down the road, so we begin to doubt what we've already begun to accomplish. Our world seems darker and our days seem shorter; things are not the way we intended for them to be. We had this plan when we were released from prison, but now everything is looking twisted and we are not getting all of our needs met.

We probably expected everything to happen all at once, but this isn't the way it happens. We may not be ready for everything all at once to happen for us because this could throw us the opposite way and cause us to want to drink, drug, or thug again. *Don't look for too much, too soon. Just keep on doing what you need to do and let things come to you along the way.*

Matthew 6:33 — *But seek ye first the Kingdom of God, and his righteousness; and all these things shall be added unto you.*

Now I Have Purpose

As soon as your spiritual eyes are open, you find your purpose in life. You may be called by God to work with children in Sunday school or visit the sick in the hospital or their homes. God knows how to use you to your full potential so that people around you can see God in you which will point them to God for themselves. How far you allow God to take you and use you is according to your level of faith in Him for what He can do with you and through you.

As long as you're doing all you know within your heart to do, God will be your strength even if you get weak at times. Being used by God to help show others the life, light, and love of Jesus builds your faith. *With God leading, you can't go wrong because you understand that you're really not in control of much of anything, but God is.*

I Timothy 4:14 — *Do not neglect your gift*

Notes from Book Four: Their Feelings

*Book Five
Hope*

Debrief Them: It's What's Needed

It is possible to change and become all we can be so that we can accomplish all we need to accomplish to be blessed and be a blessing. When we were children we didn't like everything our parent told us, made us do, or stopped us from doing. But as the parent they knew their responsibility was to help us make it to adulthood and be the best we were able to be. They knew things we didn't know and they could tell what the outcome would be if we did certain things or went a certain place they wouldn't allow.

It's not what we really wanted as children; to always be told what to do or say and where to go. But when we're older and look back, we know they did the right thing and we begin to act the same way towards our children.

Changing from the criminal master mind you tried so hard to be all your life is needed and God is the parent that can direct us in this time where we need to change. *Allowing ourselves the opportunity to live a much fuller, happier, joyful, and spirit-filled life, is showing love and appreciation to ourselves and allows others to desire the same chance to experience true living.*

Ephesians 4:22 — *You were taught, with regard to your former way of life, to put off your old self*

Love for Self

A love for self doesn't have anything to do with obtaining material things. It's the inside person within us pouring out actions that prove there's a reason to love self. When you begin to love yourself, it's hard for others not to love you.

Have a strong sense of self-worth and respect for yourself and you'll be seen by others as one draped in gold. God made only one of you and He took His time forming you in your mother's womb. He knew you before that and called you by name. This is the God who wants you to love yourself so that you can learn to love others, even your enemies.

Love starts at home within you before it can be poured out of you. For example; if someone asked you for a few slices of bread, you'd first have to have some bread before you can give some to another. *Loving yourself is necessary to move on towards a better future.*

I John 4:18 — *There is no fear in love.*

Live for God

As I wake up thinking about God's business and not be so focused on my own agenda, I find peace in serving others around me. I do things I wasn't use to doing, like meeting my neighbors, kissing my wife, and being a help to others. This kind of compassion fills the void in my heart and gives a new meaning to life.

God is in the business of saving lives and rescuing souls from sin, darkness, hatred, and hell. God brings an abundance of life that will bring about love and happiness for the rest of your life. This doesn't mean that every part of your natural life won't have its disappointments and let downs; what it does mean is that you have more strength to deal with them because of the godly attributes you have within your heart and mind.

You can go through the worst of times with joy, happiness, and love inside of you when you live for God.

Revelation 21:5 — *And He that sat upon the throne said, Behold, I make all things new*

Everyone Makes Mistakes

We are human, we are fallible (able to fail) and born in sin. This is our natural existence which makes us all imperfect. We were born in sin but we don't have to remain in sin. We can strive to be more like Jesus Christ; to walk as He walked, to love as He loves, and to forgive others as He has forgiven us.

A man of God can fall seven times and get up and continue praising, believing, and following after God. We can learn from our mistakes and become stronger in our faith in God and in our desire to be all we can be for Him and for those He has placed in our lives.

Life, love, and light is an inheritance from our Father God through our forefather, Adam, who fell from God's kingdom but obtained it back when Jesus did what He did on the cross. So, even if we make mistakes, as long as we don't continue making the same mistakes and try to do the best we know to do, we'll make it.

As we lift up Jesus, He will lift us up. If you make the wrong choices, just begin lifting Him up by praying and He'll take you through your trials and failures. *You are not silly or clumsy; you are a child of God.*

John 5:26 — *For as the Father has life in Himself; so has he given to the Son to have life in Himself*

You're a Jewel

I believe God looks upon us as His holy treasure and sees each one of us shinning and sparkling with our own personal glow. Jesus always spoke of treasures in heaven where moth or decay can't eat it, rust won't form on it, and thieves can't steal it. Jesus may have been talking about the loved ones we've lost to the grave who are waiting for us in heaven and will be there to meet us when we get there. *All I know is, God doesn't see us the way we see ourselves, but He sees our real beauty and sees us as the glorious creations He formed us to be.*

John 5:19 — *Then answered Jesus and said unto them, Verily, verily, I say unto you, The Son can do nothing of Himself, but what He seeth the Father do:*

I Have a Future

If you want a better future, you will have to make preparations for one before you're released from prison. Set little goals rather than big ones, like getting your GED so that you won't have that standing in your way of getting a decent job or going to college. Or begin exercising if you don't already do that, or learn about eating right so that you'll be healthy or healthier than you have been.

Other little goals would include things like finding out ahead of time where the community action agencies are in the city you'll be released to. Ask family members to find out some information for you about these agencies or about re-entry programs that may be available for you. The bottom line is that if you fail to plan, you plan to fail. There's help available for you, so don't miss the boat by not trying to plan for your release. It's never too late for improvement, do what it takes to improve your life; the way you dress, act, think about self and others, and the way you talk (like you have some sense). As we do what it takes to succeed in life, we set an example for others to follow. *We don't simply exist, we should live life to its fullest and be a blessing.*

Ephesians 5:29 — *After all, no one ever hated his own body, but he feeds and cares for it*

Why Can't You Look Me in the Eyes

"My love and compassion run so deep for you, and every time I look into your beautiful eyes I see the person who's so gentle and so sweet; and I wonder how I could have caused you the pain of being a drunk, a failure, a prisoner, and any other wrong I've caused. When I look deep into your eyes I see you still love me and just from knowing that, gratitude runs through my veins for you. But I don't want you to see it there, I want you to see it in every little thing I can do for you and with you."

Forgiveness is the beginning of spiritual growth when you see that a man or woman will go through it all and still be moved with compassion over you. This is when you know that a person is a real companion for life, because they have stood in your corner and had your back like a close friend. So when you can't look that person in the eyes, it may be because you're afraid that either they may see your vulnerability or you're trying not to see the hurt you may have caused.

We only caused hurt because of the bad choices we made from the lack of knowing our true purpose in life and not feeling the confidence in ourselves as we should have. We were known for pushing those we love to the limit to test their love for us. Even God doesn't want to be tested. He said He loved us and it's up to us to believe it, knowing all He has done for us by allowing His one and only Begotten Son to die in our place when He hadn't sinned and didn't deserve it.

If our mate has told and showed us love, we have the choice to believe it or not; but it's not their duty to prove it any more than they have. What is love?

I John 5:10-11 — *Herein is love, not that we loved God, but that He loved us, and sent His Son to be the propitiation (owner) for our sins. Beloved, if God so loved us, we ought also to love one another.*

Say You Need Me

Some of us got high because we felt we unneeded when our mate didn't tell or show us they were glad we were around or that they needed. We weren't given the chance to help out with the children, paying the bills, fixing things, and most of all being allowed to prove personal and private love. And it even seemed that the children didn't want to listen unless you went crazy, which doesn't help keep life simple and calm.

Maybe we were gone for too long and didn't give ourselves or our family time to form a trusting, loving relationship with us. Even when we were physically home, we may not have been mentally and emotionally supportive towards those who lives we were in. And then, to get locked up and physically removed from them, this drove an even larger wedge (space) between us.

Now that we're home we just need to be consistent in doing what it takes to prove our true intentions towards them and earn our right to be a steady part of their lives, giving them space to know and trust us.

When you show them that you need them, this changes the atmosphere in the household. Because, even if they don't say they need you, they always did need you to be there for them. And, it doesn't really matter who pays the bills in the house, as long as they're getting paid and you're contributing as a responsible family member.

Being needed is to be proven by everyone in the house.

Romans 10:12 — *For there is no difference between the Jew and the Greek; for the same Lord over all is rich unto all that call upon Him.*

My Mate Is Still Shy

Sometimes you can't watch us too closely or we become the person inside the person. It's like not having any more tricks to amuse our mate until they stand back so that we can put a trick together. Our mates must give us space to be amusing because we want to continue to see them laugh and have a good time with us. We also have to be left alone at times to deal with the shame of past experiences and situations.

We may not know how to talk about our feelings because of our childish insecurities (being too tall, too short, having big feet, not feeling as smart as others), or just not feeling that we're worthy of any good thing. Insecurities can make us doubt that we deserve the wonderful mate in front of us and makes us wonder if they have their glasses on right when they look at us.

The thing is, we can't change our looks, what happened in the past, or why our mate chose to remain with us. What we can change is our schooling situation, how we feel about ourselves, and the way we present ourselves in front of others. We can share our feelings on paper if we find it hard to share them verbally.

The more schooling and reading you allow yourself to get, the more secure you begin to feel and the better you're able to communicate to others.

Love yourself enough to make your life better and love your mate enough to prove your desire to change your inability (what you can't do) into ability (what you can do).

I Peter 3:12 — *For the eyes of the Lord are over the righteous, and His ears are open to their prayers*

Think About Others

I found out in my research that if you think about others, it lessens the stress on yourself. If we begin to get bogged down with all the things we're involved in, we should concentrate on what we can do for others. If you really want something good in life, you should give something good to others. What you give away comes back to you in blessings, gratitude, and love.

Even if the only thing you can do right now is pray for others, this is the best thing you can do. You can watch God moving upon their lives as you pray for them. They may not even know that you are praying for them, but one day you may get a chance to tell them about how you've watched God protect and bless them because you have prayed for them. Praying for others and blessing them in the ways you can, really does bring them to a point of gratefulness towards God and it also builds up your faith in God.

Faith to faith; a stair step to a higher calling in God leading you to eventually lead the lost and hopeless to Christ Jesus.

I John 2:10 — *He that loves his brother abides in the light, and there is no occasion to stumble*

Your Children Still Love You

An ex-offender may hear that their children are acting up at home by smoking, getting high and being sexually active at an age when they should be concentrating on child-like concerns like getting through school. You need to know that a child is a victim of their environment. If all they've seen are adults doing those things or adults still living as children, then what does anyone expect from the real children? They become what they know and see.

If we want them to have a better chance at life we have to present a better lifestyle to them. Because some children have been left to care for themselves, they don't really understand as much about life as they think they do and they may even act out hate for authority figures. Their hatred is really a way of them saying that they hate the fact they couldn't lean on us as a parent in their corner.

If should show our children a change in us and then give them time to see it and realize that it's permanent. We have to allow them a chance to relocate the love for us they felt they lost, and they can only do this when they can see a reason to trust us. *Every child needs a parent for guidance, including us.*

Philippians 2:13 — *For it is God which worketh in you both to will and to do His good pleasure.*

You Can Be Anything

You may have been told that you would never be anything by someone you trusted. Yet you accomplished some things on your own with a little self-esteem and motivation. If only there were those who told you something good, you wouldn't have had to struggle most of your life with trying to understand who you are.

When we hear things like, "you're smart," "you're good looking," or "you'll amount to something in life," it gives us the desire to prove others right and become all they say we can be. But if all we've heard in life is negativity, we want to prove them right and be what that negative person.

The problem is that those who were the negative influences in our lives didn't know how to be positive, because they were saying to their children what was said to them. This negative outlook on life has to end somewhere and should start with us. We can change the way we see our lives which will change the way we influence our own children's lives. We can be anything we want to be and so can our children. *We can express it by proving those wrong who thought we couldn't or wouldn't amount to anything. Give your children the same opportunity.*

I Peter 2:15 — *For it is God's will that by doing good you should silence the ignorant talk of foolish men.*

Those Days Are Over

Those were the good ole days when we were young and full of ambition and had the willingness to take on anything that presented itself to us. Life has been a challenge and its okay to look back on some things, but it's not okay to stay back there. You have to move on, pick up the pieces of your life and change the way you put them back together. We can't look back on what we didn't do or did too much of, and base our future on that. No, we have to move forward and beyond those days and get beyond holding grudges for those who have disappointed us.

We have to forgive ourselves and others; then we can move on. You can only use your past mistakes as a message to others that things can change for us. As you move forward you can be a leader for others to follow out of the past and into the future. Your message of getting beyond your mistakes can help others.

The devil lost again because you weren't ruined by the past and have moved on to a much better today and brighter tomorrow.

Galatians 3:26 — *For you are all the children of God by faith in Christ Jesus.*

You Are Not Alone

So many times we think that someone may be all alone in their misery because of a divorce, a death in the family, or hurt from a close friend. These are everyday things happening all across the world in every nation, tribe, and community. God doesn't cause these problems but He can get us through them.

People get to choose how they want to live. It's us who cause many of the problems in our lives because of our choices. In life there is good and evil, light and darkness, joy and pain. How would we know what's good if we never experienced bad? How would we learn valuable lessons in life if we didn't have some troubles? How can we relate to others going through pain if we've never hurt?

If we endure the unpleasant side of life, we become so much stronger and end up doing what we were created to do; we survive.

The Word of God says that there is a season for everything; a time to weep and a time of joy; a time to live and a time to die. We need a balance in our lives to remain stable. We need to understand that we aren't God and don't have all the answers. It allows us the opportunity to trust more in God and live like we're only in this world on a temporary basis. We can make the best of each day as God prepares for us our place in heaven which is our eternal home.

When you really begin to realize that we should live as though each day is our last, we're not afraid of much and can get through all the troubles (divorce, money problems, etc.). Having more faith in God than what's going on around you, helps to put life in the proper perspective because God can restore anything we've lost and make sure that we receive something better than we had.

Continue to enjoy the good days and remember them when you're going through the bad days.

Revelation 19:11 — *And I saw heaven opened, and behold a white horse; and He that sat upon him was called Faithful and True*

God Doesn't Make Trash

God created (spoke into being) the heavens and the earth and He saw that it was good. God formed (gently molded and made) man and woman from the dust of the ground and breathed His breath of life into them. The dust of the ground was a substance (something you can see and touch) that laid void (unused) and dormant for millions of years because it was the earth under God's construction.

God didn't form a piece of junk when He formed man and woman, you and I. We used our own selves as trash cans by filling our minds and bodies with all the evil we indulged in. If we would be more selective in what we allow ourselves to see, hear, drink, and take into our mind; we would be more positive, happy, loving, and healthy. Even prescribed medicine isn't the perfect answer to the unhealthy body we most often helped to create. What many don't realize is that prescribed medicine can relieve one symptom while causing another.

The best thing we can do is to fill ourselves up with the right things and naturally take care of ourselves even if we have to begin right now. We can't change our past, but we can change past behaviors by doing all it takes to treat our bodies and minds in the way God created us to.

Respect yourself enough to want the best for yourself. Love yourself enough to treat your mind, body and soul importantly.

Colossians 1:12 — *Giving thanks unto the Father, which hath made us meet to be partakers of the inheritance of the saints in light*

I'm Only Trying to Help

Been there, done that. Parents do try to explain to their children the outcome of certain actions and unwise choices. We want to make our children look at our mistakes and realize that if they don't want the same troubles, they shouldn't do what we did. If we could only get them to see that we were once young, and all the bad choices we made doesn't have to be made by them. Then they could use us as an example of what not to do.

Even if our children don't seem like their listening to us, as we continue to do the right things they will eventually see the truth and want to follow our leading. The problem is that they followed our lead when we were involved in the wrong things. This is why it's certain to affect them when we make up our minds to do some right things. *It takes patience to allow them to get where we finally got to in our changed behaviors, just like we had to see others changed before we made our choice to change.*

James 4:8 — *Draw near to God and He will draw near to you. Cleanse your hands, ye sinners; and purify your hearts, ye double minded.*

Shake Hands and Come Out Living

You're not a scholar and life has many twists and turns that you'll continue to go through which will make you stronger in the long run and a little smarter. You need to realize that you're not alone and you can't do it all by yourself. You need help and guidance from above so that you can get through the twists and turns of life without getting too bruised up. And just so that you don't become callused within your heart because of past wrong doings, you can always begin today to make some right choices.

I pray that this book will help be a guide to you as you begin to desire to make some changes in your life. Through this book God desires to reveal His heart of love for you as I also would like to reveal my heart to you.

The heart is where the deepest change should take place because a man's life is lived from the motives of his heart. *Once we begin making choices in life that will allow our hearts to become more positive, every part of our life changes.*

So, let's shake hands and come out living.

I Peter 4:7 — *But the end of all things is at hand; be ye therefore sober, and watch unto prayer.*

My Testimony

I want to share with you my visitation of the presence of the Lord. I raised my hand to give my life to the Lord in 1988 in a time I really needed companionship. Since then I've backslid lots of times, knowing I had a calling on my life, but ran away from God's calling as fast as I could to the liquor store for more relief.

I ended up in prison for something I didn't think they sent a man to prison for, but by the second time I went to prison I realized my life was really saved. Yes, prison had saved me from death because I had committed a B&E (breaking and entry) but the police got to me before the owner of the house did. I was drunk and out of it for 2 days before they could take my fingerprints and take me out of the restraint suit they had me in.

While in prison the second time I began studying the Bible and completing Christian studies by mail through church courses. All the time I was locked up I sought after God's face, even when I didn't feel like it. I knew that after I got the best job and roommates, and received other blessings whenever I prayed, that there must be a God who's looking out for me. It wasn't because of me that I kept on being blessed, so I decided to do God's work and He just kept on doing mine. I told people about Jesus and Jesus told His Father about me, and we've had each-other's back every since.

I went to bed one night after studying, it had been two years. I dreamed that I was in church and I was sitting in the 3rd row and was holding both of my hands over my mouth because my mind was telling me that I could preach like the preacher and I didn't want to. I heard the preaching but I didn't see anyone on the platform. Then all of a sudden words started pouring out of my mouth and I was the one on the platform preaching. I woke up and rolled off my bunk onto the floor. I ended up on my knees crying my eyes out and the presence of God was all around me, filling the room and energizing my body. Something came over me and I loved it. It was bitter sweet because my sins were being revealed and stripped away all at the same time. I didn't want to get up off of the floor because I was feeling higher than I ever felt but was more sober than I'd ever been. I felt very strong, full of spiritual knowledge and filled with compassion for others.

My Christian friends said I was glowing so they asked me to pray over everyone and everything they could think of for the next 3 days until the glow settled within me. At first I was concerned that I wouldn't know how to hold on to this spiritual awakening, but I learned how to keep it. I just need to love everyone to keep that peace and glory alive within me until I get home to heaven where I'll experience all the glory of God.

Because of the relationship I now have with my Father God, this is why He inspired me to write this book. Not just for ex-offenders but for anyone who needs to know that even though change is a natural part of life, some change is necessary and up to each one of us to make happen. It's like choosing to pick up a book to read instead of hanging out doing the wrong thing, or choosing to forgive yourself and others for past bad choices.

This book is designed to help ex-offenders learn ways to adjust to the outside once they are released from prison, but it's also to assist those who have been locked up inside due to alcohol and drug abuse. It's to help anyone understand the family's pain that would have been caused by a loved one's bad choices.

I pray that God is able to help you become all you can be for the rest of your life.

Colossians 2:2 — *My purpose is that they may be encouraged in heart and united in love, so that they may have the full riches of complete understanding, in order that they may know the mystery of God, namely, Christ, in whom are hidden all the treasures of wisdom and knowledge.*

Notes from Book Five: Hope

Manufactured By: RR Donnelley
Breinigsville, PA USA
June, 2010